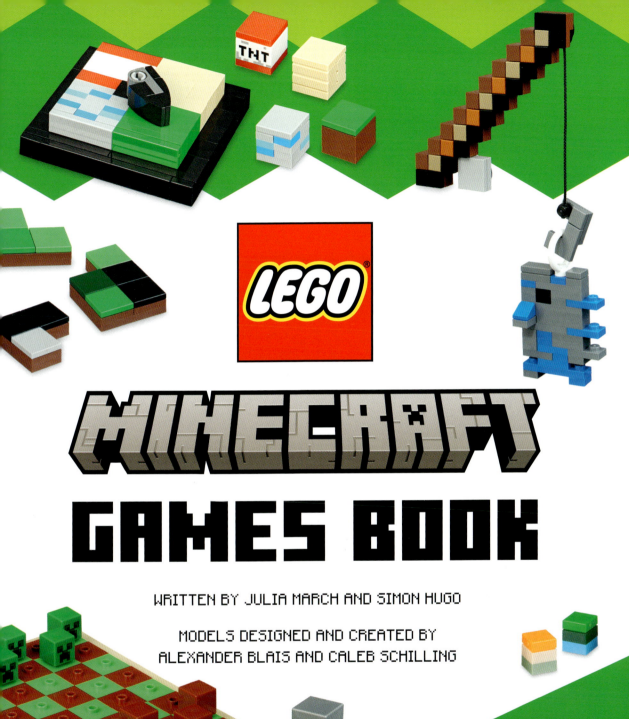

LEGO MINECRAFT GAMES BOOK

WRITTEN BY JULIA MARCH AND SIMON HUGO

MODELS DESIGNED AND CREATED BY
ALEXANDER BLAIS AND CALEB SCHILLING

DK

CONTENTS

- 8   Nether Minecart Race
- 10   Odd Block Out
- 11   Enchanting Table Challenge
- 12   Tropical Fish Pickup
- 14   Minecraft Block Sudoku
- 16   Target Practice
- 18   Micro Biome Builders
- 19   Sneaky Spot-The-Difference
- 20   Build A Minecraft House Challenge
- 22   Creeper Crash
- 24   Mining Sequence
- 25   Block Balance
- 26   Grow Wild Build-A-Thon
- 27   Spin It To Spawn It
- 28   Pig Pen Game
- 30   Minecraft Fairground
- 38   Portal Pinball
- 40   Wheel Of Fortune

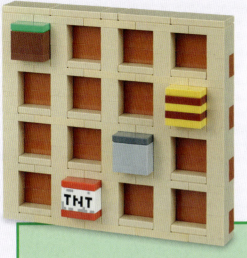
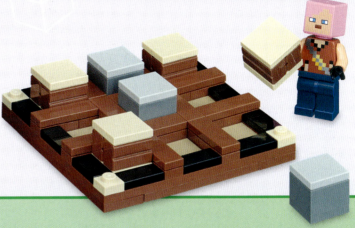

41	Micro Model Challenge
42	Navigate The Nether
44	Creeper Jigsaw Puzzle
46	Pickax Mining Race
47	First Night Challenge
48	One-Element Figures
50	TNT Dash
52	Creeper Catcher
54	Map Maker
56	Terraform Challenge
58	Material Worlds
60	Keep The Light On
61	First To Four
62	Out Of The Mine, Into The Maze
64	TNT Toss
65	Memory Mosaic
66	Classic Game Selection Box
72	Panda Skee-Ball
73	Meet The LEGO® Minecraft® Designers
74	Useful Pieces
76	Acknowledgments

NETHER MINECART RACE

Race your friends through the Nether in this Minecraft obstacle course. Will you spin your way past the magma cubes and other items to be the first minecart home?

TRY THIS
For a more complex game, add places where the tracks overlap. That way players can start on one color, but move to other colors on their route to the finish line.

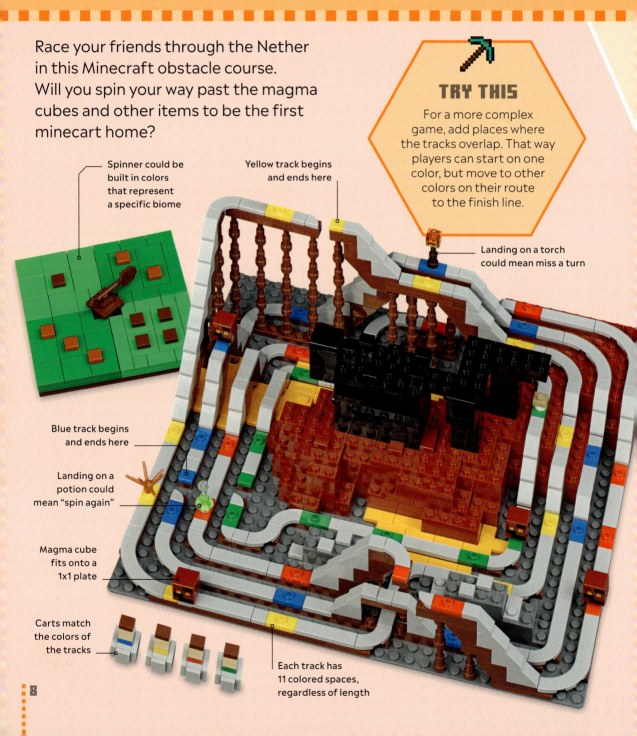

Spinner could be built in colors that represent a specific biome

Yellow track begins and ends here

Landing on a torch could mean miss a turn

Blue track begins and ends here

Landing on a potion could mean "spin again"

Magma cube fits onto a 1x1 plate

Carts match the colors of the tracks

Each track has 11 colored spaces, regardless of length

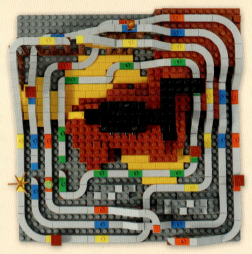
TOP VIEW

HOW TO PLAY

1 Build or draw a Nether board with four colored tracks and four matching minecarts.

2 Add one magma cube and an equal number of other items (such as fire, a potion, or a mushroom) to each track.

3 Build a spinner and decide rules for the various items: e.g. landing on a magma cube means you go back two spaces.

4 Players pick a track and take turns to move between colored pieces according to the number they spin and the items they land on. The first to do a complete loop wins.

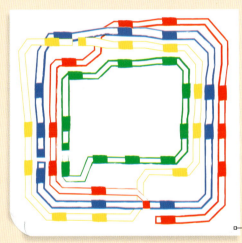

Plan your track by drawing it first—or simply use your drawing as the game board!

HOW TO BUILD

Light green 6x6 plate · Dark green 6x6 plate

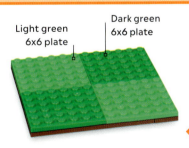

1 Overlap two layers of LEGO plates to make a 12x12 base.

2 Use 1x1 tiles to mark numbers from one to four.

2x2 jumper plate has one central knob

These parts add height so the pointer can spin freely

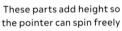
LEGO® Minecraft® shovel piece

2x2 turntable

3 Build a spinning pointer onto a 2x2 turntable in the center.

9

ODD BLOCK OUT

Six Minecraft crafting blocks, all exactly the same. Or are they? Challenge your friends to spot the single difference that makes a certain block the odd one out. They'll need to keep a crafty eye open to solve this one!

TRY THIS
Create larger blocks by using bricks instead of plates. If you make the blocks as hollow boxes with lids, you could even hide a small prize inside the odd one out!

HOW TO PLAY

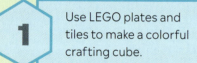

1 Use LEGO plates and tiles to make a colorful crafting cube.

2 Make four exact copies of the first cube, and one with a subtle difference.

3 Decide on rules. Can players pick the cubes up, or do they just have to move around them?

4 Finally, line up the six cubes and see who can be the first to spot the odd one out!

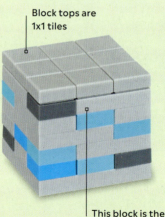

Block tops are 1x1 tiles

This block is the odd one out!

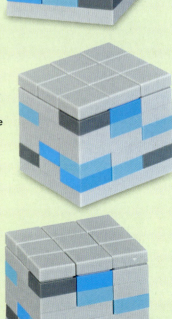

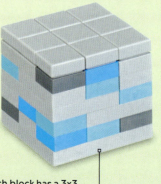

Each block has a 3x3 plate as its base

ENCHANTING TABLE CHALLENGE

UNDERSIDE VIEW

In this challenge, you have just two nimble-fingered minutes to transform a Minecraft item from ordinary to enchanted. Turn that plain pickax purple or prepare to lose it for good. (Or maybe just try again …)

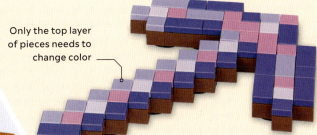

Only the top layer of pieces needs to change color

Use tile pieces for a smooth look

GLOW FOR IT!

In Minecraft, enchanted items take on a purple glow. If you're short on purple LEGO pieces, simply invent your own new enchantment colors!

HOW TO PLAY

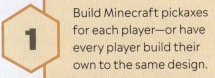

1 Build Minecraft pickaxes for each player—or have every player build their own to the same design.

2 Choose a clear surface to be your enchanting table and put all your purple LEGO pieces on it.

3 Players then sit around the pile of purple pieces and enchant their pickaxes as fast as they can!

4 The first player to make a fully enchanted pickax is the winner.

TROPICAL FISH PICKUP

This fintastic fishing game will have you hooked. The aim is to fill a Minecraft bucket with tropical fish mobs faster than other players. The catch? The fish are tiny and just waiting to slip off your hook back into their ocean biome.

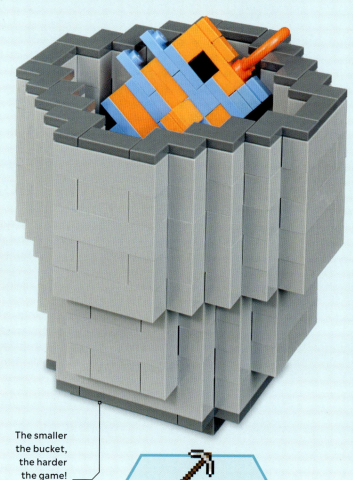

HOW TO PLAY

1 Build a Minecraft bucket and fishing rod with a hook using your LEGO collection.

2 Build five or more tropical fish, with hooped tongues for the hook to catch onto.

3 Spread the fish out and use the rod to see how many you can hook and lift into the bucket in one minute.

4 Challenge your friends to beat your haul, or see how quickly you can hook all the fish out of the bucket and back into their biome!

The smaller the bucket, the harder the game!

BUILD TIP
Try building fish with fins like cup handles instead of giving them hooped tongues. As long as they have somewhere for the hook to go, they should be catchable!

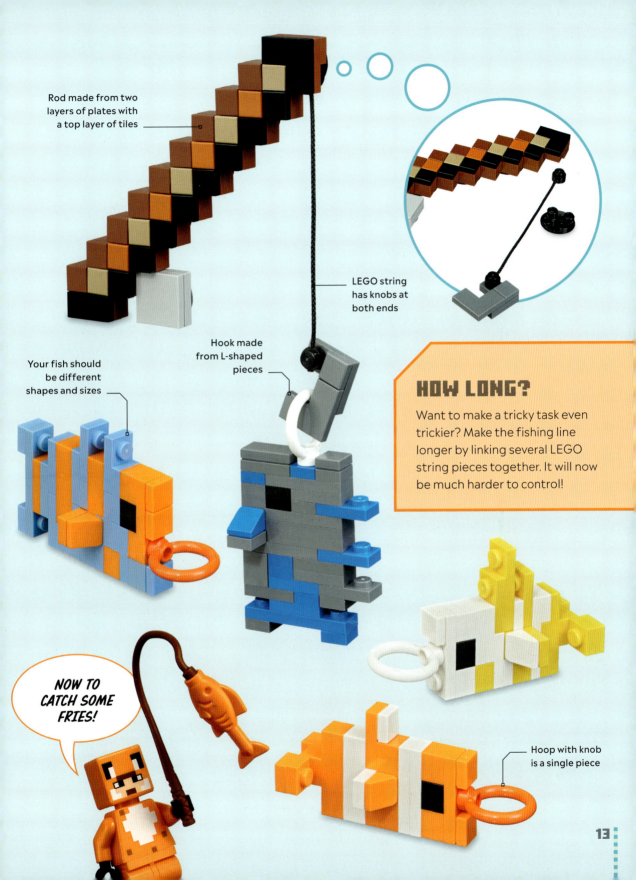

MINECRAFT BLOCK SUDOKU

There are no numbers in this sudoku game—just Minecraft blocks. You have to arrange them so there are no repeated pieces in each row and column. It's quite tricky, so build in a clue or four!

Each block is two knobs in depth

Each slot is one knob in depth

These 12 blocks need to be slotted into the grid

Each block is five LEGO plates high

The four blocks already in the grid are built in and do not move

Smooth tiles allow blocks to slide in and out

HOW TO BUILD

1 The entire build is 13 knobs wide. Build each row with one built-in block.

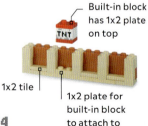

Built-in block has 1x2 plate on top

1x2 tile

1x2 plate for built-in block to attach to

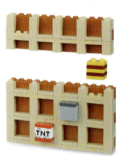

2 Build a different style of block into a different column in each row.

3 Finish with a layer of plates and a layer of smooth tiles.

HOW TO PLAY

1 The aim of the game is to fill in the grid so that no row or column has more than one of each block type.

2 The built-in blocks cannot be moved, and so rule out certain solutions. See them as clues, not obstacles!

3 Challenge your friends to solve the puzzle. Whoever does it in the fastest time gets to build the next one!

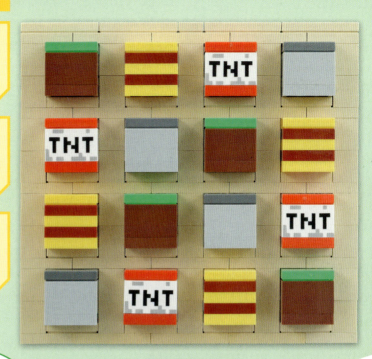

SOLUTION

DO YOU SUDOKU? SO DO I!

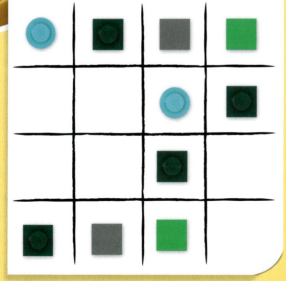

TRY THIS

If you're impatient to get going, forget building and play sudoku on paper instead. Just draw a 4x4 grid on a piece of paper and use four groups of four matching LEGO elements as playing pieces.

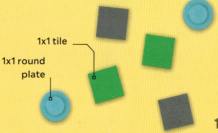

1x1 tile

1x1 round plate

TARGET PRACTICE

These Minecraft targets won't give off redstone signals when you hit them, but they will win you valuable points. Take your position on the wall and try to hit all three with your LEGO launcher. Ready, aim, fire!

I'M GIVING IT MY BEST SHOT!

Built-in shooter fires 1x1 round plates

Shooting platform slides back and forth along smooth tiles

1x2 plate with rail slots into bricks with grooves

TRY THIS

Targets will look even more like Minecraft ones if you build them as cubes. You could make them in different sizes so some are harder to hit than others. Award points according to difficulty.

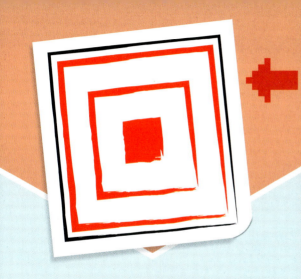

PAPER TARGETS

Paper targets will work just as well as LEGO ones, and you can still use LEGO bricks to support them. Alternatively, lay your targets flat, so the round plates come to rest on them.

Minecraft bullseyes are square!

Targets angled using hinge bricks

HOW TO PLAY

1 Build a launch platform with a built-in shooter (see below) and three targets.

2 Put the targets in a safe place in front of the launcher. Try a few practice shots and adjust the target positions if needed.

3 Take turns with friends to fire 1x1 round plates from the shooter, earning a point each time you hit a target.

4 Players can slide the shooter back and forth along the launch platform, but must not move the platform itself!

HOW TO BUILD

Smooth 2x4 tile

1x4 brick with groove

2 The moving platform is built separately, with a built-in launcher.

1x3 jumper plate for Steve to stand on

Built-in shooter

1x2 plate with rail

1x1 plate

1x2 plate with rail

1 The base of the launcher has a smooth, tiled surface on top of two back-to-back rows of bricks with grooves.

3 Plates with rails are built onto the underside of the platform and slot into the bricks with grooves.

MICRO BIOME BUILDERS

This game tests your building skills and your biome smarts! With just a handful of pieces, you must make something that is from or represents a particular Minecraft setting. Then, the other players have to guess which biome your micro model belongs to!

TRY THIS

You don't have to build an actual part of the biome, like the frozen taiga river below. Be imaginative. A chicken shouts (or clucks) "plains" because that's where many Minecraft farms are.

This chicken knows where it's from!

HOW TO PLAY

 1 Write the names of several Minecraft biomes on slips of paper and put them in a bag.

 2 Each player takes a random piece of paper from the bag, but doesn't reveal what it is.

3 Players now have 10 minutes to make a model that represents their biome. No peeking at others just yet!

 4 Finally, players present their models and take turns to guess which biomes other people have built.

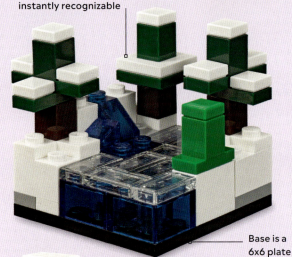

This build is small but instantly recognizable

Base is a 6x6 plate

KEEP IT TINY

What counts as micro? Agree on a size limit before you start. You could say objects must fit onto a 6x6 baseplate, or limit the number of elements that may be used.

SNEAKY SPOT-THE-DIFFERENCE

Steve must have a twin brother, right? Wrong! There are four small differences between these two figures. Build your own not-quite-matching pair, then challenge your friends to spot the differences.

BUILD TIP
These Steves are built with jointed legs, so they can be placed in walking and sitting poses. Just like minifigures, the tops of their legs are not flat. If they were, they could not rotate.

Collar is more open on this figure

Eyes are a darker shade

This Steve's sleeves are one plate shorter

Gray shoes instead of black ones

HOW TO PLAY

1 Build two identical Minecraft figures from LEGO pieces.

2 Change a few of the details on figure two. Don't make the changes too obvious.

3 Challenge a friend to find the differences. Be kind and tell them how many there are!

4 When your friend has found all the differences, they can build the next pair of lookalikes.

19

BUILD A MINECRAFT HOUSE CHALLENGE

Imagine you are a Minecraft minifigure house-hunting in the Overworld. What would your dream home be? In this game, a slip of paper decides for you. All you have to do is build it ... using LEGO bricks, of course.

Sideways bricks built onto bracket plates

Printed bee tile found in several LEGO Minecraft sets

TREE HOUSE

BUILD TIP

Not every LEGO house has to be built at minifigure scale. When time or pieces are limited, building in microscale can make a little go a long way. An entire microscale house might have fewer than 10 parts!

WHAT ARE THE NEIGHBORS LIKE?

SNOW CABIN

Stray mobs are right at home in snowy biomes

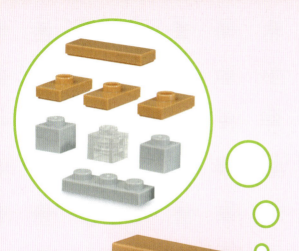

ADOPT AND ADAPT

For a different challenge, swap houses at the end of the game. Then play again, with everyone adapting another player's build to fit a new set of styles.

Just 11 pieces make this plains village house

MICROSCALE BUILDING

HOW TO PLAY

1 Each player takes a slip of paper, writes down an idea for a house style, and then puts it in a shared bag.

2 Players choose an idea at random from the bag. If you choose your own idea, put it back and try again!

3 For the next 20 minutes, everyone builds a house in their chosen style—without revealing what that style is!

4 When the time is up, try to guess each other's style, and share friendly tips on home improvement!

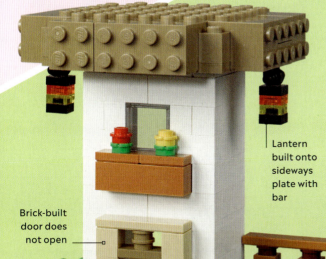

Lantern built onto sideways plate with bar

Brick-built door does not open

MUSHROOM MANSION

THEY'RE TOTAL BLOCKHEADS!

21

CREEPER CRASH

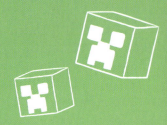

Don't fear the creepers! In this tabletop bowling alley you can send the hostile mobs flying before they get a chance to creep up on you. See if you can take out all 10 with one well-aimed ball.

1x2 bases make the creepers harder to knock over

TRY THIS

For a bigger challenge, make your bowling alley wider and add gutters all along both sides. If the ball falls into one of these sunken channels before it reaches the creepers, your turn is over!

CREEPER PINS

HOW TO BUILD

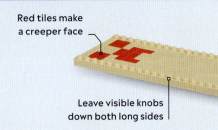

Red tiles make a creeper face

Leave visible knobs down both long sides

Use smooth tiles in the center

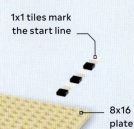

1x1 tiles mark the start line

8x16 plate

1 Use plates and tiles to build an alley that is 48 knobs long and 8 knobs wide.

HOW TO PLAY

1 Set up 10 creeper pins in a triangle shape at one end of the bowling alley.

2 Place a LEGO ball at the other end of the alley and set it rolling with a flick.

3 Count how many creepers your ball knocks down, and score a point for each. Then set the creepers up again.

4 Take turns like this and keep a running total of your score. The winner is the first player to reach 50 points.

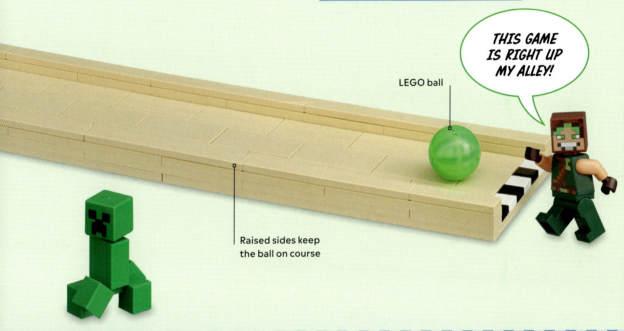

THIS GAME IS RIGHT UP MY ALLEY!

LEGO ball

Raised sides keep the ball on course

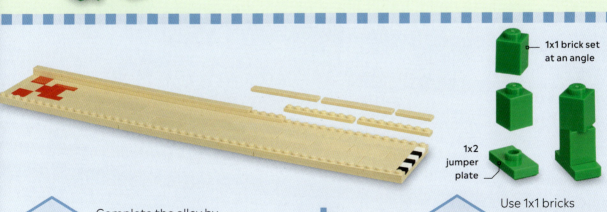

1x1 brick set at an angle

1x2 jumper plate

2 Complete the alley by building low walls along both long sides.

3 Use 1x1 bricks and jumper plates to make 10 identical pins.

MINING SEQUENCE

Use your mind to figure out what's been mined. Ask a friend to lay out a sequence of different LEGO mined objects in a recognizable pattern. Can you figure out which colors and shapes you must add to continue the sequence?

HOW TO PLAY

1 Player one lays out a sequence of LEGO pieces that could be mined items.

2 Using logic, player two adds the next few pieces that they believe continue the sequence.

3 When player two gets the pattern right, players switch roles.

Make sure to leave the correct pieces in a pile for the player to choose from

The blue piece will follow this dark-green piece

COME ON ... IT'S OBVIOUS

ER ... NOT TO ME, PAL!

PICKED OUT PARTS

Another way of playing is to lay out a sequence with some gaps in it and challenge a friend to fill in the missing pieces. The idea is exactly the same.

24

BLOCK BALANCE

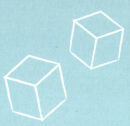

They're going ... they're going! This crafting table has a built-in wobble that makes it hard to stack blocks on. See how many blocks you can stack before they all come tumbling down.

Smooth-topped blocks are not attached to each other

Obsidian block

Bee nest block

Top half pivots on LEGO® Technic axle pins

Gap between top and bottom allows for movement

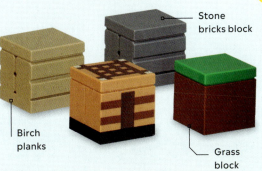

Stone bricks block

Birch planks

Grass block

HOW TO PLAY

1 Build blocks and a crafting table with a top half that tilts back and forth.

2 Players take turns to stack blocks on the table, one block at a time.

3 The player whose move makes one or more blocks fall is out.

4 The other players start again. Play on until just one is left—the winner!

25

GROW WILD BUILD-A-THON

Build crops and beat the clock in this challenge. Who can make the most mini Minecraft plants with their LEGO collection? Start the timer and get growing to find out!

HOW TO PLAY

1 Spread out a pile of LEGO elements and set a timer for two minutes.

2 Players must try to build the best mini plant model they can before the time is up.

2 After two minutes, everyone compares their builds and agrees upon a winner.

Attach tiles to 1x1 brick with four side knobs to make a chorus flower

2x2 round jumper plate for petals

Stack flower stems to create a rosebush

Treetop built in same way as chorus flower

1x1 round bricks look like sugarcane

1x1 half-circle tiles form part of a lily pad

Knobs create a spiky cactus look

LEVEL UP!

Add more time to the clock and work together to create a life-size plant instead. Will you flourish?

SPIN IT TO SPAWN IT

In this game you can spawn new mob members, you can be gifted them, or you can lose them. It all depends on how the spinner falls. Will you be the mightiest mob master in town, or will you end up empty-handed?

HOW TO PLAY

1 Each player builds five micro mobs of their choice. You will also need to make a spinner.

2 Players take turns to use the spinner. What number will the pointer land on?

3 If you spin a one, miss a turn. For two, give a mob to another player. For three, discard a mob. For four, take a mob from the discard pile (if there are any to take).

4 The game ends when one player is out of mobs. The player with the most mobs at this stage wins.

See p.9 for how to build

BUILD TIP

Unsure what a 1x1 brick with side knob is? Need to check the difference between a LEGO tile and a LEGO plate? You can use your "Useful Pieces" guide on pp.74–75 and take your building to another level!

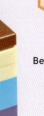
Steve micro mob is a stack of 1x1 pieces

Bee built like Steve, but sideways!

Llama is made using three 1x1 bricks with side knob

Sheep has knobs all around for a woolly look

Chicken is built around a single headlight brick

PIG PEN GAME

Put your farming skills to the test with this Minecraft pig-wrangling game inspired by the ancient African game Mancala. You'll use strategy to shoo pig counters into the pen. Careful though—if any pigs escape, you lose. It's enough to make you squeal with frustration!

HOLD THAT PIG!
Remember, once a pig is in the pen, there it stays. Don't move it again. All the other counters will continue moving until the game is over.

HOW TO PLAY

1 Draw a grid, as below, with a pink section for the pen. Put two pigs (LEGO pieces) into each section, apart from the pen.

2 Take pigs from any section and drop them into those ahead—one per section until they run out.

3 If the last pig drops into an empty section, unless it's the pen, you're out. If it drops into the pen, repeat step 2.

4 If the last pig in your hand drops into a section with other pigs, you must collect those pigs and drop one into each section ahead. You win when you pen all of the pigs.

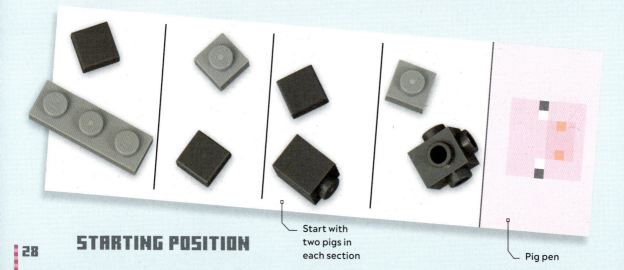

STARTING POSITION

Start with two pigs in each section

Pig pen

In this game there's no way to avoid dropping a pig into an empty section

LOSING PIG PEN

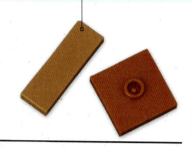

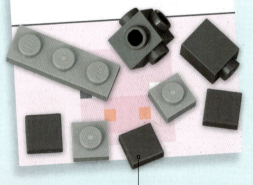

All of the pigs are in the pig pen

WINNING PIG PEN

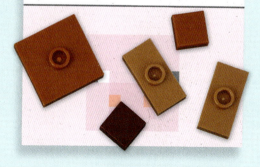

29

MINECRAFT FAIRGROUND

Roll up! Roll up! Enjoy all the fun of the fair at the Minecraft fairground. These side stall games will test your skill and your luck. Why not offer a Minecraft minifigure or a model you've made as a prize?

Hinge bricks hold rails on at an angle

Use pieces no larger than this 2x2 jumper plate

HOW TO PLAY

1 Build a minecart as a bucket. Set it up on a sloping piece of track so it's at an angle.

2 Gather a selection of LEGO pieces, all small enough to fit in the minecart bucket.

3 Players take turns to throw the LEGO pieces into the bucket. If one bounces out, they can't throw it again.

4 After each player's turn, jot down how many pieces are in the bucket. Top scorer wins the game. If it's a tie, organize a bounce-off!

CHUCK IT IN THE BUCKET!

BRICK IN A BUCKET BOUNCE

Who can get the most bricks into an angled bucket without them bouncing out? The steeper the angle, the greater the bounce risk.

30

HOW TO PLAY

1 Build six Minecraft chickens. From above, they must look identical.

2 Use colored LEGO pieces underneath the chickens to mark them as pairs.

3 Players take turns to match the pairs. Be sure to shuffle the chickens well after every turn.

4 The player who matches the most pairs wins. If anyone gets them all ... well, it must be their clucky day!

PICK A CHICK

Mix the chicks and put your memory to the test in this matching game. Who will end up with the most matches?

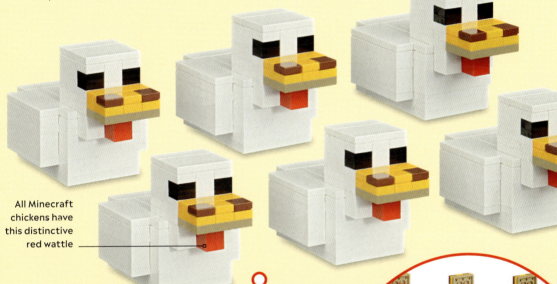

All Minecraft chickens have this distinctive red wattle

TRY THIS

Play a game of chance instead. Make the undersides of five of the chickens white. One chicken gets a colorful plate underneath. The player who chooses the colorful bird at random wins a prize!

UNDERSIDE VIEW

RING TOSS

This game is sometimes called "hoopla." If you can throw a ring over a prize, you win it. For your Minecraft fairground, the ring is more of a square!

Large iceberg in frozen ocean

Pointed dripstone stalagmites

MINIFIGURE SCALE FAIRGROUND RIDE

Ferris wheel, roller coaster, or carousel? Send your mobs up, down, and all around with a thrilling minifigure-scale fairground ride. Hold on tight!

Gold dotted throughout mine

HOW TO PLAY

1 Write the names of different fairground rides on slips of paper.

2 Shake the bag, then pull out just one of the slips.

3 Players join forces to build a Minecraft version of the ride. It must be big enough for a minifigure to fit on.

4 There's no winner in this challenge—except perhaps for the lucky minifigure that gets to try out the ride!

MAKE A MOVE

Aim to build a ride that really moves. This minecart roller coaster is right on track! Minecarts might also work as dodgems or Ferris wheel pods.

HOW TO PLAY

1 Create a few micro builds of Minecraft objects. Tall and narrow is best.

2 Build a square "ring" out of LEGO pieces, large enough to encircle each object.

3 Players each have five tries to throw the ring over one or more objects.

4 You don't have to give your micro builds as prizes. Just award the top scorer the title of "ringmaster."

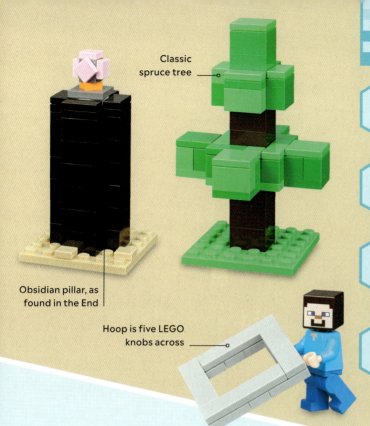

Classic spruce tree

Obsidian pillar, as found in the End

Hoop is five LEGO knobs across

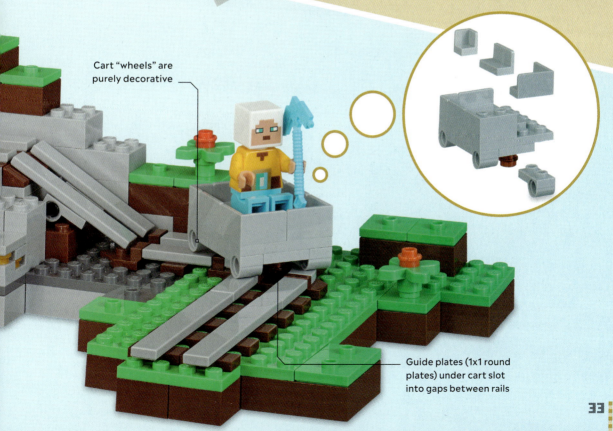

Cart "wheels" are purely decorative

Guide plates (1x1 round plates) under cart slot into gaps between rails

33

WHACK-A-MOB

Those pesky mobs just keep popping up everywhere. Bash them down with this Minecraft version of the classic whack-a-mole game.

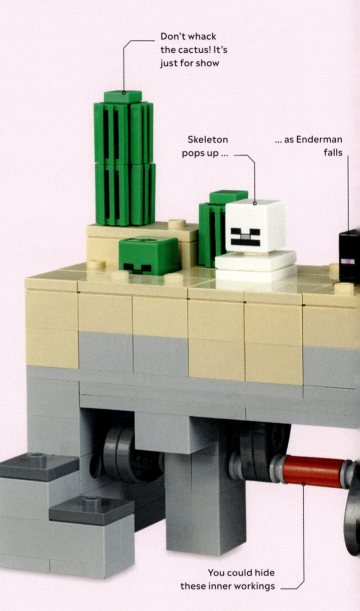

Don't whack the cactus! It's just for show

Skeleton pops up ...

... as Enderman falls

You could hide these inner workings

HOW TO PLAY

1 Build the whack-a-mob machine and hammer.

2 Pick a player to turn the handle that makes the mobs pop up and down.

3 Players have 30 seconds each to bash the up-popping mobs.

4 The player who made the most hits wins. How about a box of popcorn as a pop-up prize?

BUILD TIP

Builds with moving parts can be the most challenging to make. Don't worry if your whack-a-mob game doesn't work the first time. Learning from trial and error is even more rewarding than getting things right immediately!

MISS-A-MOB

Make it harder by including one "friendly" mob that players must avoid hitting. If they accidentally hit it in their hammering frenzy, they lose a point.

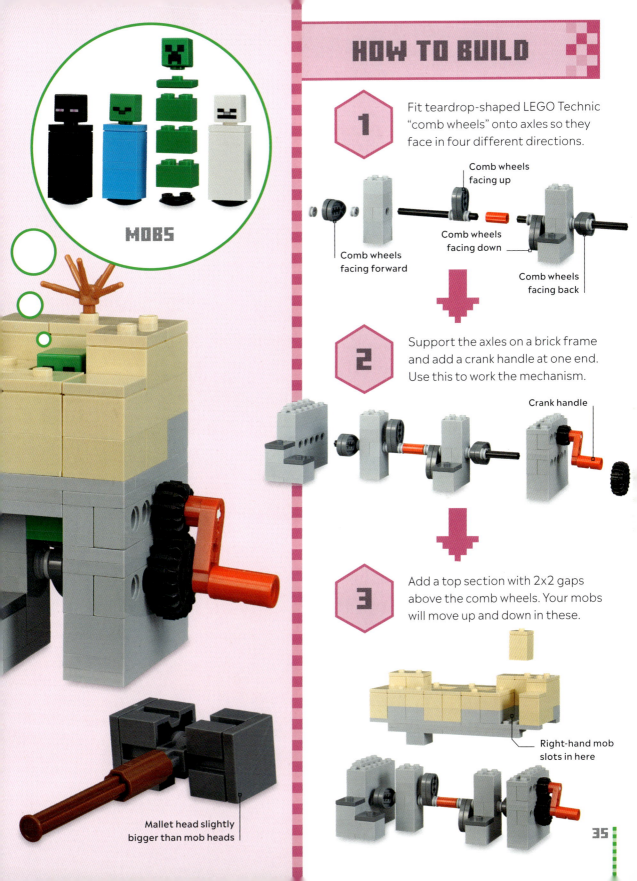

MOBS

HOW TO BUILD

1 Fit teardrop-shaped LEGO Technic "comb wheels" onto axles so they face in four different directions.

Comb wheels facing forward
Comb wheels facing up
Comb wheels facing down
Comb wheels facing back

2 Support the axles on a brick frame and add a crank handle at one end. Use this to work the mechanism.

Crank handle

3 Add a top section with 2x2 gaps above the comb wheels. Your mobs will move up and down in these.

Right-hand mob slots in here

Mallet head slightly bigger than mob heads

35

HOW TO PLAY

1 Find a transparent jar or other container.

2 Fill the jar with a jumble of LEGO pieces. Remember to write down how many first!

3 Ask your friends to guess how many pieces are in the jar. They mustn't touch.

4 The winner is the person whose guess is closest to the actual number.

GUESS THE NUMBER OF ELEMENTS

How many LEGO pieces in the jar? That's for players to guess! Make the game extra competitive by including a highly desirable element in the jar as a prize.

Use a premade container, or build one from transparent LEGO pieces

Each pumpkin is three LEGO knobs wide and deep

KNOCK THE CAN

This game is stacks of fun. It's a can knock-down game, but with grinning pumpkins instead of cans. Knock them back to their home biome!

HOW TO PLAY

1 Build six Minecraft carved pumpkins and stack them as shown.

2 Players take turns to hurl a LEGO ball at the stack, with three throws each.

3 Whoever knocks down the most pumpkins in three throws wins—by a knockout.

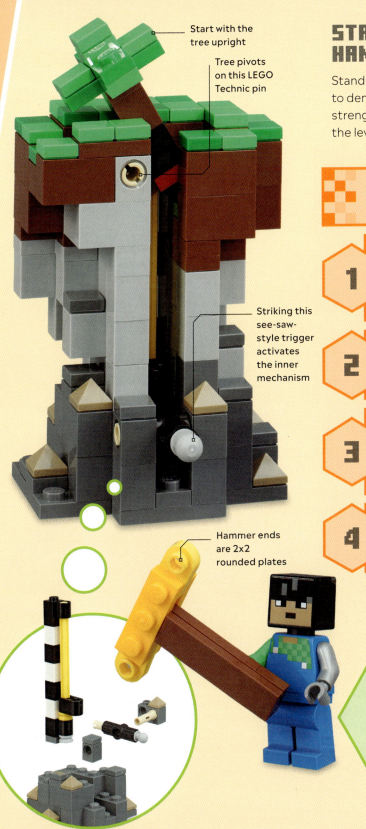

Start with the tree upright

Tree pivots on this LEGO Technic pin

Striking this see-saw-style trigger activates the inner mechanism

Hammer ends are 2x2 rounded plates

STRENGTH TEST HAMMER GAME

Stand back, everyone—it's time for you to demonstrate your tree-mendous strength. Smash the hammer down on the lever and watch the tree topple.

HOW TO PLAY

1 Build a cross section of the Minecraft earth—rock, soil, and grass—with a central vertical channel.

2 A shaft through the channel connects a lever at the bottom to a swiveling tree at the top.

3 Players take turns to hit the lever with the hammer, trying to make the tree fall. It usually takes several attempts.

4 The player who fells the tree in the fewest tries is the winner. Timbe-e-e-er!

BUILD TIP

This is a chain-reaction build. Striking the trigger at its base causes a small LEGO Technic beam to move up its core. If the beam reaches the top, it causes the tree to topple. Keep this sequence in mind as you build.

PORTAL PINBALL

Become a pinball wizard—Minecraft style! Set the ball rolling and use the flippers to whack it up the board. Will you make it to the End portal, or will the bumpers bounce you back again ... and again ... and again?

THAT YELLOW ROUND THING IS THE WEIRDEST BLOCK I'VE EVER SEEN!

TILT TO WIN

Another way to make a handheld ball game is to make a mazelike ball run. Instead of using flippers to move the ball, you just tilt the entire build from side to side.

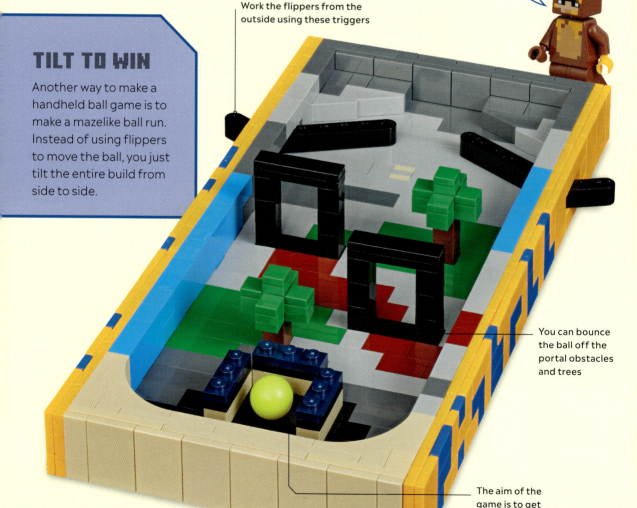

Work the flippers from the outside using these triggers

You can bounce the ball off the portal obstacles and trees

The aim of the game is to get the ball in here

38

HOW TO PLAY

1 Hold the game in both hands, with your thumbs on the triggers so the ball rests on the flippers.

2 Launch the ball by pressing down fast on one or both of the triggers.

3 Aim for the U-shaped End portal. You'll have to get through one of the arches or portal obstacles to score.

4 Use the flippers to keep the ball in play every time it bounces back from one of the obstacles. If you get the ball into the top portal, you win. If the ball drops below the flippers, you lose!

BUILD TIP
Think of the playing surface of this game as a LEGO wall, lying flat on its back. You can build it upright and then lay it down, or you can build the whole thing sideways!

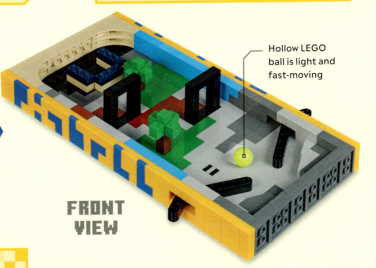

Hollow LEGO ball is light and fast-moving

FRONT VIEW

HOW TO BUILD

LEGO Technic angle beam pivots on gray LEGO Technic pin

LEGO Technic pin fits into sideways brick with hole

Build the mid section with different biome colors and places to attach obstacles.

Side decorations attach to bricks with side knobs

Use LEGO Technic half pins in bricks with holes to attach the End portal

1 Start by building the trigger end of the game. Each trigger/flipper is a LEGO Technic angle beam.

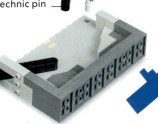

1x1 brick with side knob

2

3 Add a goal at the top and decoration on the sides. Don't forget to add obstacles too!

WHEEL OF FORTUNE

This four-player game can be just for fun, but it's also useful for when you need to make Minecraft decisions. Why not use the wheel to decide who goes first in a game, or which block to base your next build on? Give it a whirl!

HOW TO PLAY

1 Build a square "wheel" representing four familiar Minecraft blocks.

2 Make four Minecraft blocks that match the squares on the wheel.

3 Put the blocks into a bag. Each player picks one out at random.

4 Give the pointer a flick to spin it. Whichever block it lands on is the winner.

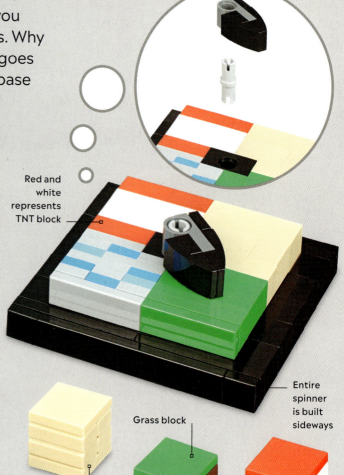

Red and white represents TNT block

Entire spinner is built sideways

Birch planks

Grass block

1x2 brick with printed TNT design

Diamond ore block

WHEEL IT BE YOU?

This game also works in reverse. Spin the wheel first to decide the lucky block, then take turns to see who will draw the winning block from the bag.

40

MICRO MODEL CHALLENGE

Candle made from two pieces

Cow has three pieces

This challenge is tiny but tough. You have five minutes to build a recognizable Minecraft object from just a few LEGO pieces. What will yours be? A mini mob, a teeny tree, or a bitsy building perhaps.

HOW TO PLAY

1 Lay out a selection of your smallest LEGO pieces and get players to gather round.

2 Players have five minutes to make as many tiny builds as possible, taking pieces from the selection one at a time. No hoarding allowed!

Micro Alex vs. zombie mob

Tree has 10 pieces

3 When the time is up, players guess what each other's builds are. A correct guess earns a point for the guesser and the builder.

TRY THIS

Set a maximum number of pieces that players can use in each micro build, or challenge players to make one three-brick build, one four-brick build, one five-brick build, and so on.

Savanna village house

4 When the guessing is over, the person with the most points is named the winner.

Plains village house

NAVIGATE THE NETHER

This Nether escape board game will have you all fired up. Hop over lava and rocks to flee the dangerous realm, but beware! Land on a portal and you'll have to linger longer in the lava.

Use differently colored 1x1 bricks as playing pieces

The first player to reach this finish line is the winner

FINISH

Each jumper plate is a space on the path

If you land on a portal you miss a turn

Players can only land on the jumper plates

Start here

START

42

TRY THIS

A path through the Nether is just the beginning! For a real challenge, add micro mobs such as Endermen, hoglins, and ghasts to the route and come up with different penalties for landing on them.

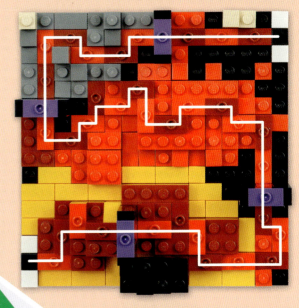

OVERHEAD VIEW

Build your own spinner on p.9

I THOUGHT I'D NETHER GET OUT!

HOW TO PLAY

 Build a game board with a path made from LEGO jumper plates, some of them set on top of portals.

 Playing in rounds, players spin the spinner and move their piece the number of spaces shown, from one to four. Each jumper plate counts as a space.

 If you land on top of a portal, bad luck! You must miss a turn while your playing piece goes on a dimensional journey!

 The first player to make it safely to the end of the path wins. But you must spin the exact number to get there!

43

CREEPER JIGSAW PUZZLE

Solve this Minecraft jigsaw and you'll come face to face with a creeper. Yikes! Don't worry—this LEGO creeper isn't going to explode. You'll have to take the puzzle apart yourself when you've finished it.

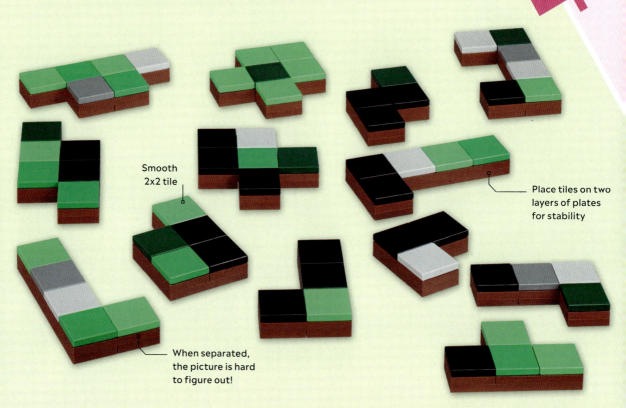

Smooth 2x2 tile

Place tiles on two layers of plates for stability

When separated, the picture is hard to figure out!

HOW TO PLAY

1 Design a square creeper face made from LEGO tiles that sit on your "jigsaw" pieces.

2 Scatter all your jigsaw pieces on a flat surface. Try to assemble the creeper face as fast as you can.

3 Challenge your friends to complete the puzzle faster than you!

Use tiles, plates, or a mix of both to make your picture

Make this same puzzle at half the size using 1x1 pieces

SAY "CREEPER"

Take a photo of your completed build before you scatter the pieces for the first time. Let players look at the picture if they struggle to solve the puzzle without it.

HOW TO BUILD

1 Create your jigsaw pieces by arranging LEGO pieces into small shapes that combine to make one large square.

2 Build your picture on top of the pieces with colored flat tiles or plates.

Colored flat tiles make a picture when pushed together

45

PICKAX MINING RACE

In this game, you must mine your chosen ore from a jumble of LEGO elements. You have just 30 seconds and can only use a LEGO Minecraft pickax to do it. Which ore will you choose? Take your pick!

I LOVE THIS LEGO AX-ESSORY

Each "mined" pile must be a different color

Use pieces no larger than these 2x2 jumper plates

HOW TO PLAY

1 Put a handful of small LEGO pieces into a pile, making sure there are an equal number of each color. These are your ores.

2 Using only a minifigure pickax, players have 30 seconds to mine ores of one color out of the pile.

3 Players can take turns, or all play at once, having agreed in advance which color ore each person will collect.

4 When the time is up, the winner is the person who has removed the most ore from the pile.

ORE OR NOTHING

If a player adds an ore of the wrong color to their pile, it doesn't count toward their final haul. Perhaps it even loses them a point!

FIRST NIGHT CHALLENGE

Imagine you've landed in a brand-new Minecraft world. You're alone and helpless—no food, no shelter, no anything! Can you build all you need to survive your first night?

A lit furnace is always useful!

Apple built flat like a mosaic

Torch made from 1x1 bricks and 2x2 plates

TRY THIS
This is not a points game and there doesn't need to be a clear winner. Players might not all agree on who has the best builds, but seeing how people approach building challenges in different ways is all part of the fun.

HOW TO PLAY

1 Players gather round a large pile of LEGO pieces and start a 15-minute timer (or keep an eye on a clock).

2 Before the time runs out, players must build a shelter; something to eat; and two other useful items.

3 Builds can be minifigure scale, or any size you like, but use your time wisely!

4 When the time is up, players compare their builds to see who has the best chance of making it through the night!

47

ONE-ELEMENT FIGURES

Is it possible to build a recognizable Minecraft skin using just one LEGO element? It is if you use lots of that one element! All of these builds are made using the same-shaped piece, in different colors, over and over again.

TRY THIS
This challenge also works well with Minecraft animals. Try building single-element cats, llamas, pigs, frogs, axolotls, and rabbits. You could even build a single-element Ender Dragon!

HOW TO PLAY

1 Look through your LEGO pieces to see which elements you have plenty of.

2 Challenge yourself or others to make a Minecraft skin using just one of these piece types. Set a timer, if you like.

3 When your build is finished, show it to other Minecrafters to see if they can recognize it.

HEY, YOU'RE NEW ROUND HERE!

This Alex is made from 2x2 round plates

Standard 2x2 plates make this Steve

This Alex is made from 1x1 plates

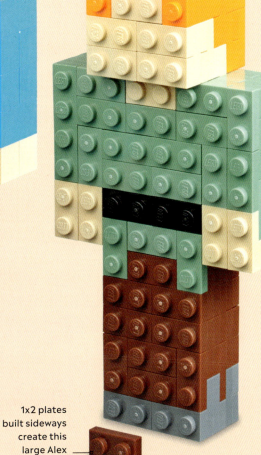

The same six colors are used to build all three Alex figures

BUILDING US? IT'S ELEMENTARY

Steve is made from just five colors

1x2 bricks stack up to form this large Steve

1x2 plates built sideways create this large Alex

BUILD TIP

These builds are all about capturing the basics of a skin rather than the details. Looking at skins through half-closed eyes can help you filter out detail and get a more general sense of shape and color.

TILE FIGURES

You can even play this game using LEGO tiles, which don't have knobs! Simply arrange the loose pieces like a mosaic on a flat surface.

49

TNT DASH

Draw bricks from a bag to pick your way through this explosive Minecraft board game. Colorful bricks tell you which square to hop to next, while white ones send you back to the beginning with a bang!

Playing pieces start off the board

PLAYING PIECE

White brick is TNT

This player drew a blue brick

START

HOW TO PLAY

 1 Fill a bag with bricks matching the colors of the squares on your playing board, plus a few bricks of another color (e.g. white) to represent TNT.

 3 If the nearest square of your chosen color is behind you, move backward. If you draw a TNT brick—kaboom!—you go back to the start.

2 Players take turns to draw a brick from the bag, moving their playing piece to the nearest square of that color.

 4 The winner is the first player to reach the end.

BUILD TIP

The black squares on the board below are topped with grille pieces. These work just as well as tiles, since they also lack knobs and playing pieces cannot become attached to them by mistake.

HOW TO BUILD

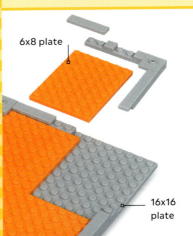

6x8 plate

16x16 plate

Use overlapping plates to make a 16x16 playing board.

2x2 tile

1x2 grille

2x2 plate

Make a colorful, winding pathway of 2x2 squares across the board.

The first player to reach this square is the winner

FINISH

THIS GAME IS SUCH A BLAST!

1x2 brick with printed TNT design

Add decorations such as TNT blocks to the board corners.

CREEPER CATCHER

In this game, one player controls a team of six heroes and the other leads a team of six creepers. Each side tries to trap the other, and the winner gets to play the heroes next time. You just need to decide who'll play the creepers in the first round!

TRY THIS
You don't have to use 1x1 plates for the counters, as shown here. If you make the board a little bigger you could use black 1x3 plates or replace playing pieces with LEGO Minecraft minifigures and mob figures.

HOW TO PLAY
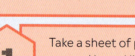

1 Take a sheet of paper and draw a round board like the one shown here.

2 Position six dark-green playing pieces and six light-green ones as shown on the right (any small LEGO pieces will do).

3 Dark-green goes first, moving any one of their pieces to its nearest empty intersection (where two lines meet).

4 Players take turns to move in this way, trying to surround their opponent's pieces, one at a time, on all sides.

5 When a piece is surrounded so it cannot move in any direction, it is taken out of play. The game is won by capturing four of your opponent's pieces.

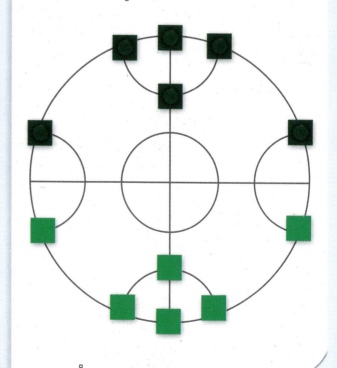

Player one sits on this side of the board

Player two sits on this side

STARTING POSITION

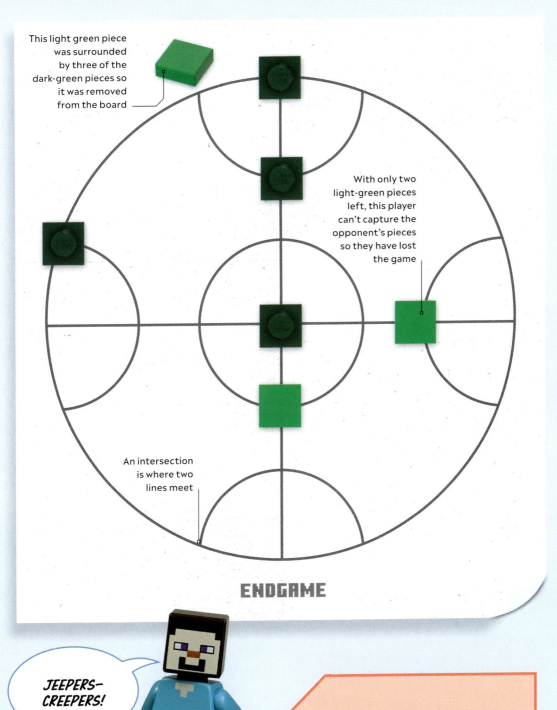

ENDGAME

JEEPERS-CREEPERS!

MADE FROM MELONS

This Creeper Catcher is based on a Chinese game called "watermelon chess." The circular board is a melon and the counters are its seeds.

MAP MAKER

Some days it can be hard deciding what to build and where. This game does the deciding for you, putting you and your friends on course to make a nine-biome map as fate decrees. There are no winners or losers—just blocky building teamwork!

HOW TO PLAY

1 Write nine Minecraft biome names on slips of paper and then fold them up so you can't see what they say.

2 Divide a larger piece of paper into nine squares and put one folded slip on each square at random.

3 Each player takes a slip and looks at it to see what kind of biome they need to build on their chosen square.

4 When a player finishes a build, they place it on its square, take another slip, and start building again.

5 When all nine squares are built on, your Minecraft map is complete.

It's all mushroom fields around here!

54

The slip of paper on this square said to build a badlands model

STARTING VIEW

BUILD TIP
Starting with one micro biome already built in the middle of the map can help your fellow crafters judge the scale of their own builds. This will result in a more unified looking map.

I REMEMBER WHEN ALL THIS WAS PAPER!

Greenery on a blue base means this is a swamp biome

55

TERRAFORM CHALLENGE

Bored with your biome? Maybe it's time to pull a switcheroo—LEGO style. Modify a model by swapping a few details and changing the colors. You'll turn that birch grove into a mushroom field in no time!

HOW TO PLAY

1 Choose your favorite LEGO Minecraft set, or build a new model from scratch.

2 Think about how the build would look different if it was set in another biome—and what would look the same.

3 Adapt the build (or make a copy) so it keeps its overall shape and size, but clearly looks like an all-new biome.

4 Challenge your friends to do the same with their favorite LEGO Minecraft sets.

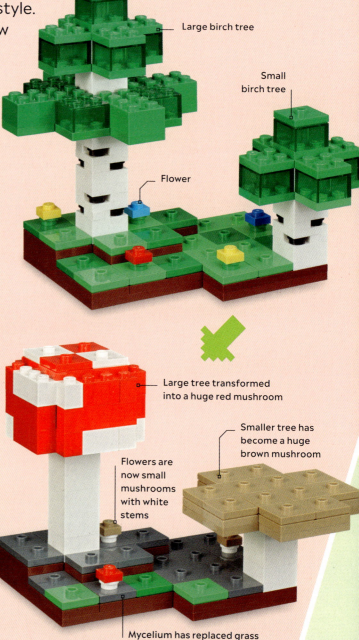

Large birch tree

Small birch tree

Flower

Large tree transformed into a huge red mushroom

Smaller tree has become a huge brown mushroom

Flowers are now small mushrooms with white stems

Mycelium has replaced grass

56

TRY THIS

Not all LEGO sets are LEGO Minecraft sets. Take a build from another LEGO play theme (such as LEGO® Friends or LEGO® City) and give it a Minecraft makeover!

Birch tree

Slime

I WISH IT WERE WARMER.

Huge crimson fungus

Coal ore

Magma cube

Refreshing waterfall

TOO WARM!

NOW OR NETHER

This scene has taken a trip from the Overworld to the Nether. Keeping the Steve minifigure in the same place and pose helps show that it is two alternative takes on the same build.

Nether gold ore

Fiery lava fall

57

MATERIAL WORLDS

With a little imagination, LEGO elements can be any material you like. In this game, players pull random LEGO Minecraft blocks out of a bag and make them the basis for a world of brilliant builds!

HOW TO PLAY

 1 Make a selection of Minecraft blocks representing different materials and put them in a bag.

 2 Without looking, players take one block each from the bag.

 3 Players then have 20 minutes to build something using the colors from their selected block.

 4 When the time is up, players compare their builds and vote for the winning creation.

BIRCH PLANKS

SNOW LAYERS

GRASS BLOCK

LAVA

DIAMOND ORE

OBSIDIAN

MOSSY COBBLESTONE

KEEP THE LIGHT ON

Imagine being stuck in the dark with a creeper. If you let your torch go out, that's exactly what might happen in this chilling game of chance. Shudder! You'll need a cookie piece, a flame brick, and a whole lot of luck.

HOW TO PLAY

 1 Take turns tossing the cookie piece (or a similar one from your collection).

 2 If the cookie lands printed side down, extinguish the flame in the flame brick.

 3 If it lands printed side (or knob side if using a brick) up, "relight" the flame or leave it lit.

 4 Play for 10 rounds and keep note of how many times your flames go out.

 5 The player with their torch lit for the most rounds is the winner. The loser has to face the creepers!

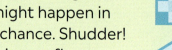

Add the flame when you win your toss

Remove the flame piece when you lose a toss

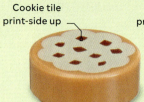

Cookie tile print-side up

Cookie tile print-side down

FEAR THE DARK

In Minecraft, creepers spawn in dark places. A lit torch—or even a flame like this LEGO piece—can keep their numbers down.

BUILD TIP

Maybe you don't have the cookie piece handy. No worries, just flip any flat LEGO element with different-looking sides.

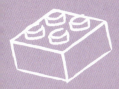 

FIRST TO FOUR

This game is played with just two colors, but many shades of strategic thinking! Build up and build out for as long as you can, until one player lines up four bricks of their color in a row.

HOW TO PLAY

1 Both players start with a pile of 2x2 bricks in a single color of their choice.

2 Player one puts down one brick. Player two adds a brick on top to start a tower, or right beside it, to start a wall.

3 Players continue to lay one brick per turn, building as wide and tall as they like.

4 The first player to make a line of four bricks in their color (horizontally, vertically, or diagonally) without being blocked is the winner.

BLOCK THE BLOCKS

Players can use their bricks to block their opponent's color row in its tracks! If that happens you'll need to move in a different direction or start a new row from scratch.

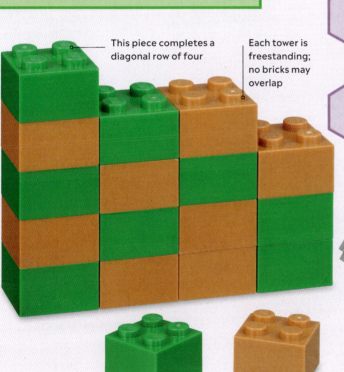

This piece completes a diagonal row of four

Each tower is freestanding; no bricks may overlap

2x2 brick

I DEMAND A YELLOW TEAM!

OUT OF THE MINE, INTO THE MAZE

This mining maze game has twists and turns aplenty. You and your friends have mined a piece of lapis lazuli … Yay! But who can get it out of the mine and through the surrounding forest in the fastest time? Grab your pickaxes and let's find out!

TRY THIS
There is only one route through the maze shown, but it can be easily adapted with very little rebuilding. Simply lift out the trees and relocate them to create a whole new route in just a few seconds!

START — Place the round lapis lazuli plate here to begin

THAT WAS A-MAZE-INGLY FAST!

Blue 1x1 round plate represents lapis lazuli

FINISH — Stop the stopwatch when the lapis lazuli piece comes out here

THE BEST OF TIMES

You don't need all your friends around at once to play this game. Draw (or build) a scoreboard to keep a record of their best times over days or weeks.

HOW TO PLAY

1 Build a maze with a mine at one end and a way out at the other. Be sure to include some dead ends! Place a 1x1 round plate in the mine as lapis lazuli.

2 Challenge your friends to move the mineral out of the mine and through the maze using only a minifigure pickax.

3 Players must not pick the maze up, but they can keep it steady with their other hand.

4 Use a stopwatch to see which of your friends can complete the challenge in the fastest time.

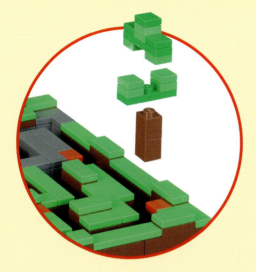

Maze measures 16 knobs square

OVERHEAD VIEW

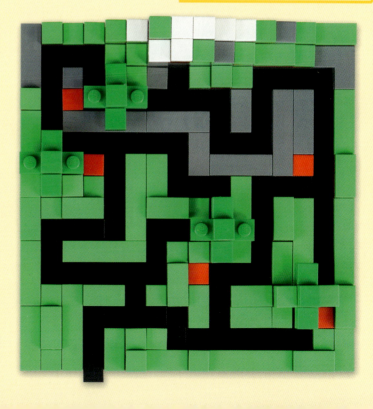

TNT TOSS

Are you a safe pair of hands? Then you'll love this Minecraft version of the "hot potato" game. Don't let the block hit the ground or you'll blow the TNT (and your chances of winning).

HOW TO PLAY

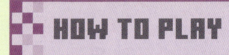

1 Build a large TNT block from LEGO pieces. Form a circle with your friends.

2 Start tossing the TNT around the circle, faster and faster.

3 Drop the TNT and you're out! The last person left becomes the TNTTC (the TNT tossing champion).

LOOK OUT ... IT'S GONNA BLOW!

Top of "T" is a 1x1 plate

Lettering mostly made from sideways 1x2 plates

64

MEMORY MOSAIC

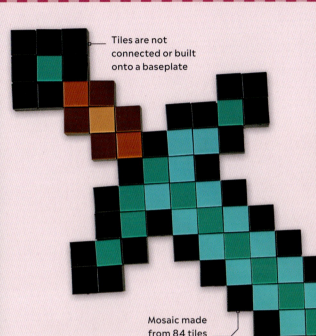

Tiles are not connected or built onto a baseplate

Mosaic made from 84 tiles

Build a mosaic of a Minecraft object by laying your LEGO pieces into a shape. Beautiful, huh? Take a minute to admire your work. Better make that two minutes, because now you have to rebuild it from memory. You might wish you hadn't made your design so complex!

SHARP SWORD, SHARP MEMORY

HOW TO PLAY

1 Lay out the shape of a diamond sword (or other Minecraft item) in LEGO pieces.

2 Take a photo and hide it. Break up the mosaic and try to rebuild it from memory.

3 You have just 20 minutes. Did you get it right? Check the photo.

BUILD TIP

Smooth, square tiles make the most traditional-looking mosaics, but the majority of LEGO elements can be laid out to form a flat picture. Experiment with various shapes for different artistic effects.

65

CLASSIC GAME SELECTION BOX

These classic games have been around since Minecraft was a twinkle in a mob's eye. They've stood the test of time for a reason. Grab your LEGO pieces and bring a Minecraft twist to some all-time favorites.

TIC-TAC-TOE

The aim of this game is to fill an entire row with your color while blocking your opponent from doing the same. It's simple, yet tic-tac-totally tricky.

You will need five blocks of each color

Smooth, tiled base stops blocks from sticking

TRY THIS

Give some not-so-classic variants a try. In scramble tic-tac-toe, both players can use both colors. Or how about reverse tic-tac-toe, where the aim is to *avoid* getting three in a row.

Not all blocks will be used in every game

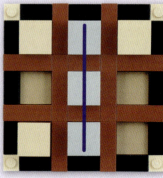

WINNING ROW

HOW TO PLAY

1 This is a two-player game. Build a square frame with holes for nine blocks and blocks to fit inside.

2 Players take turns adding blocks of their color to the frame.

3 The winner is the first player to line up three of their colors in any direction.

CHECKERS

This two-player game will capture your attention. Can you work your way across the board, capturing your opponent's mobs as you go?

HOW TO PLAY

1 Build two teams of eight checker mobs. Place them on the board as shown.

2 Players take turns moving their mobs forward, one green square at a time. Diagonals only!

3 If a player meets an enemy piece with an empty space beyond it, they can jump over the enemy piece and remove it.

4 The winner is the player who captures all of their opponent's mobs, or traps them so they can't move.

TRY THIS

The creeper heads and magma cubes shown here are only a suggestion. You can play with any LEGO pieces, as long as you have eight matching pieces for each player.

Printed creeper head piece

Printed magma cube piece

Heads attach to 2x2 jumper plates

LEGO Minecraft helmet element

CROWN THE KING!

If a piece reaches the other side of the board, it becomes a king. Now it can move diagonally forward or backward. How will you adapt it to show it's a king?

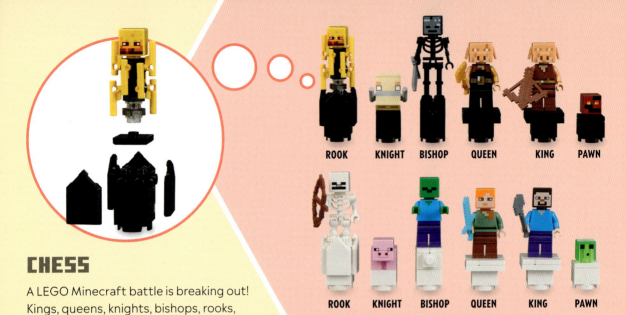

CHESS

A LEGO Minecraft battle is breaking out! Kings, queens, knights, bishops, rooks, and pawns stand ready to fight, and a checkered board is their battleground. Who will win?

ROOK **KNIGHT** **BISHOP** **QUEEN** **KING** **PAWN**

ROOK **KNIGHT** **BISHOP** **QUEEN** **KING** **PAWN**

Build 1 king, 1 queen, 2 rooks, 2 bishops, 2 knights, and 8 pawns for each LEGO Minecraft team.

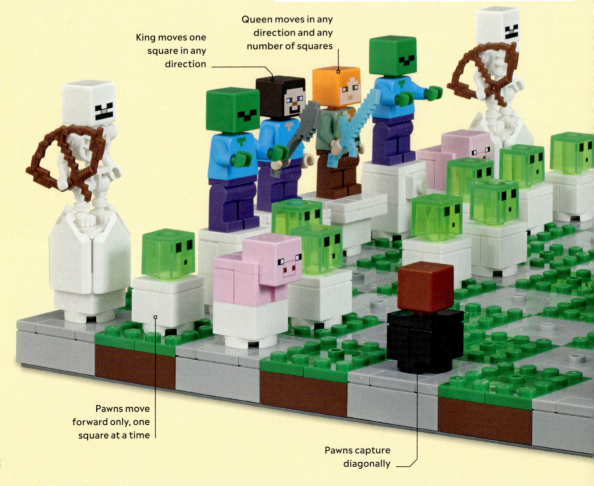

King moves one square in any direction

Queen moves in any direction and any number of squares

Pawns move forward only, one square at a time

Pawns capture diagonally

ROOK	KNIGHT	BISHOP	KING	QUEEN	BISHOP	KNIGHT	ROOK
PAWN	PAWN	PAWN	PAWN	PAWN	PAWN	PAWN	PAWN
PAWN	PAWN	PAWN	PAWN	PAWN	PAWN	PAWN	PAWN
ROOK	KNIGHT	BISHOP	KING	QUEEN	BISHOP	KNIGHT	ROOK

STARTING POSITIONS

HOW TO PLAY

1 Build a chess board with 64 squares, and team pieces for two players.

2 Players take turns to move their pieces across the board.

3 The aim is to capture the other player's king. Each piece moves in a different way, so plan ahead.

4 The game ends when one player captures the other player's king.

Bishops move diagonally any number of squares

Rooks move forward or sideways any number of squares

Knights move in an L-shape and can jump other pieces

TRY THIS

For more portable play, the checkerboard on p.67 also works as a mini chess board. Use the checker pieces as pawns and different colored 1x1 round bricks for the other pieces.

69

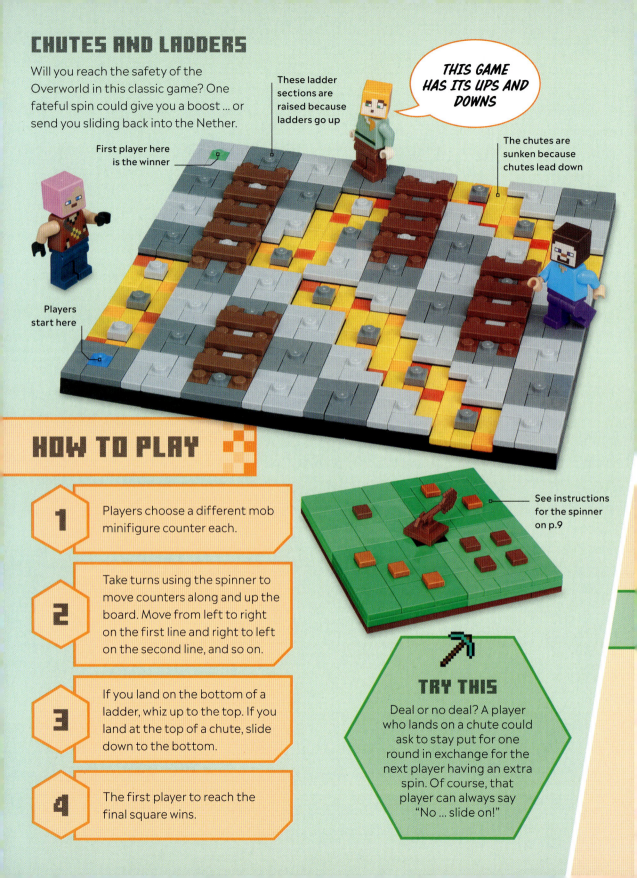

CHUTES AND LADDERS

Will you reach the safety of the Overworld in this classic game? One fateful spin could give you a boost ... or send you sliding back into the Nether.

These ladder sections are raised because ladders go up

THIS GAME HAS ITS UPS AND DOWNS

The chutes are sunken because chutes lead down

First player here is the winner

Players start here

HOW TO PLAY

1 Players choose a different mob minifigure counter each.

2 Take turns using the spinner to move counters along and up the board. Move from left to right on the first line and right to left on the second line, and so on.

3 If you land on the bottom of a ladder, whiz up to the top. If you land at the top of a chute, slide down to the bottom.

4 The first player to reach the final square wins.

See instructions for the spinner on p.9

TRY THIS

Deal or no deal? A player who lands on a chute could ask to stay put for one round in exchange for the next player having an extra spin. Of course, that player can always say "No ... slide on!"

LUDO

Victory could be just around the corner when you play LEGO Minecraft Ludo. Combine luck and strategy to bring your tokens home.

Tokens join the path on their first colored square

Pigs start in the cherry grove

Each player starts with four pieces

Zombies start in the forest

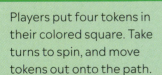

After circling the board once, zombies take this path home

HOW TO PLAY

1 Players put four tokens in their colored square. Take turns to spin, and move tokens out onto the path.

2 Move around the board clockwise on the brown, cross-shaped path—up and then down each arm.

3 You can move the same token with each spin or have all four in play. If you land on a rival token, knock it back to the start!

4 When a token has been all the way around the board, start moving it up its own colored path toward the triangle.

5 When a token reaches its own colored triangle in the center, it's "home." The first player to get all four pieces home wins.

71

PANDA SKEE-BALL

In Minecraft, playful pandas stick out their tongues. This LEGO panda has no tongue, but it does have a big, wide-open mouth. Pretend your ball is a bamboo shoot and start feeding the panda in this fun skee-ball game.

Make the open mouth slightly bigger than a LEGO ball

TRY THIS

Not wild about pandas? Don't worry—any Minecraft animal can be a skee-ball board. A cat would welcome a few well-aimed fish-balls, or try bowling apples at a hungry horse.

"Swallowed" balls land in this tray

Sloping tummy runway built using plates with clips and bars

STAND BACK, I'M ON A ROLL!

HOW TO PLAY

 1 Build a panda with a big, open mouth and a tummy that forms a slope.

 2 Players take turns to roll a LEGO ball up the slope, aiming for the mouth.

 3 Earn a point every time the ball goes into the panda's mouth. Eyes score nothing!

 4 After six rounds, add up the scores to find out who is the best (bamboo) shooter.

MEET THE LEGO® MINECRAFT® DESIGNERS

Alexander
Location: Ebeltoft, Denmark
Day job: Film student

What's your favorite model from this book?
My favorite model is the fish hook game. Fishing is one of the most fun parts of Minecraft, and I think the hook game captures that feeling.

What are your tips for building LEGO® Minecraft® models?
When building Minecraft models it is important to look at references to make models that are accurate to the game. Luckily, you can just play Minecraft to find everything in the game from any angle you need!

What's the most challenging model that you made for this book?
The most challenging model was the panda skee-ball. I really wanted to get a balance between being playable and looking as much like a Minecraft panda as possible.

Caleb
Location: Minnesota
Day job: Level designer

What's your favorite model from this book?
I had a tremendous amount of fun working on the whack-a-mob model. Adding movement to a build really takes it to the next level, and this is something I can see myself tinkering with at my desk for years to come!

What do you do when a build doesn't go according to plan?
Always be ready to improvise! It happens quite frequently that I run out of parts in a certain color. Say you don't have enough gray elements to finish your cliff wall. Perhaps you could use blue bricks to create a waterfall (or an orange lavafall!) there instead. Adding more color to a Minecraft world is always a positive in my eyes.

What's your favorite LEGO® element?
I definitely find myself using the 1x2 plate with slide a lot in my builds. It can help create some really interesting architectural dimensions, and these can help accomplish some cool shapes.

USEFUL PIECES

It can be useful to learn more about the different types of LEGO® pieces you have in your collection. You don't need all of these—just get creative with the pieces you do have!

Small parts and small balls can cause choking if swallowed. Not for children under 3 years.

BRICK BASICS
LEGO® pieces are measured by the number of knobs they have. Bricks with two knobs along and four knobs up are called 2x4 bricks. Bricks are one of the most common elements used to create all types of models.

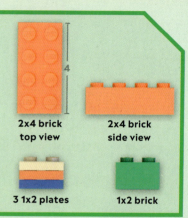

2x4 brick top view

2x4 brick side view

3 1x2 plates

1x2 brick

TILES
Tiles give models a smooth finish. Printed tiles add extra details to your builds.

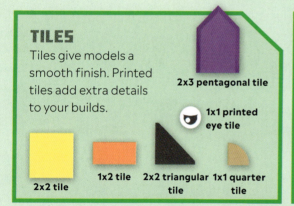

2x3 pentagonal tile

1x1 printed eye tile

2x2 tile

1x2 tile

2x2 triangular tile

1x1 quarter tile

SLOPES
Slopes have diagonal angles. They come in many different sizes. Some are inverted (upside down).

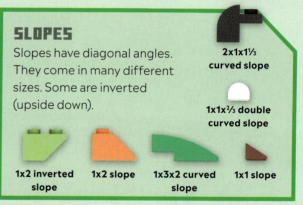

2x1x1⅓ curved slope

1x1x⅔ double curved slope

1x2 inverted slope

1x2 slope

1x3x2 curved slope

1x1 slope

PLATES
Plates have knobs on top and tubes on the bottom. Plates are thinner than bricks.

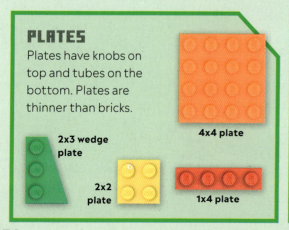

2x3 wedge plate

4x4 plate

2x2 plate

1x4 plate

CONNECTIONS
Clip and joint pieces like these add movement to models by creating flexible connections.

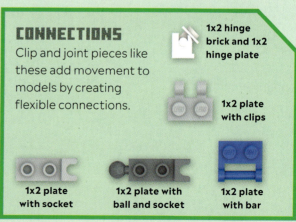

1x2 hinge brick and 1x2 hinge plate

1x2 plate with clips

1x2 plate with socket

1x2 plate with ball and socket

1x2 plate with bar

MINECRAFT PIECES

Dig out your special Minecraft pieces or look for similar elements in the same colors for a Minecraft effect.

 1x2 printed furnace brick

 2x2 printed cake tile

 1x2 textured brick

 1x2 printed TNT brick

 2x3 tile with clips Illager banner

 Printed creeper head

 Printed carved pumpkin head

 Printed Enderman head

 Printed skeleton head

 2x2 tile crafting grid

 2x3 tile shield piece

BUILD BASICS

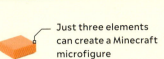

 Just three elements can create a Minecraft microfigure

 This tiny cow is made from 1x1 tiles attached to a 1x1 plate with bracket

 A simple oak tree can be formed around a 1x1 brick with knobs

 These gold brown pieces are a similar color to the acacia planks used in savanna buildings

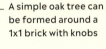 This small flame piece could be swapped for a red round 1x1 plate to make a candle

 A 2x2 jumper plate with a tile on top makes a pointed cottage roof

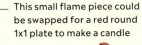

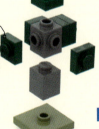 Use dark green and gray elements to create an acacia tree

Project Editors Lisa Stock and Nicole Reynolds
Designers Jenny Edwards and Isabelle Merry
Senior US Editor Megan Douglass
Managing Editor Tori Kosara
Managing Art Editor Jo Connor
Production Editor Siu Yin Chan
Senior Production Controller Lloyd Robertson
Art Director Charlotte Coulais
Publisher Paula Regan
Managing Director Mark Searle
Jacket Designer Jenny Edwards

Models designed and created by
Alexander Blais and Caleb Schilling
Photography by Gary Ombler

Dorling Kindersley would like to thank: Randi Sørensen, Heidi K. Jensen, Martin Leighton Lindhardt, Nina Koopmann, and Joseph Patrick Kyde at the LEGO Group; Lauren Marklund and Kelsey Ranallo at Mojang. DK also thanks Julia March for proofreading, Helen Murray for editorial assistance, and James McKeag for design assistance.

First American Edition, 2025
Published in the United States by DK Publishing,
a division of Penguin Random House LLC
1745 Broadway, 20th Floor, New York, NY 10019

Page design copyright © 2025 Dorling Kindersley Limited

LEGO, the LEGO logo, the Minifigure, and the Brick and
Knob configurations are trademarks of the LEGO Group.
©2025 The LEGO Group.

Manufactured by Dorling Kindersley, 20 Vauxhall Bridge Road,
London SW1V 2SA under license from the LEGO Group.

© 2025 Mojang AB. All Rights Reserved.
Minecraft, the Minecraft logo, the Mojang Studios
logo, and the Creeper logo are trademarks of the
Microsoft group of companies.

25 26 27 28 29 10 9 8 7 6 5 4 3 2 1
001–345144–July/2025

All rights reserved.
Without limiting the rights under the copyright reserved above,
no part of this publication may be reproduced, stored
in or introduced into a retrieval system, or transmitted, in any
form, or by any means (electronic, mechanical, photocopying,
recording, or otherwise), without the prior written
permission of the copyright owner.
Published in Great Britain by Dorling Kindersley Limited

ISBN 978-0-5939-6579-5
Library ISBN 978-0-5939-6698-3

Printed and bound in China

www.dk.com
www.LEGO.com

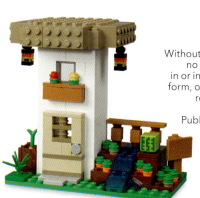